Confident,

Determined

and Caring

A Lucky Duck Book

Learning to be

Confident,

Determined

and Caring

Karen Brunskill

P·CP
Paul Chapman
Publishing

First published 2006

Originally published in Australia as Values for Life Junior Level Primary Series Two 2002

 Paul Chapman Publishing
A SAGE Publications Company
1 Oliver's Yard
55 City Road
London EC1Y 1SP

SAGE Publications Inc.
2455 Teller Road
Thousand Oaks, California 91320

SAGE Publications India Pvt Ltd.
B-42, Panchsheel Enclave
Post Box 4109
New Delhi 110 017

www.luckyduck.co.uk

Commissioning Editor: George Robinson
Editorial Team: Mel Maines, Sarah Lynch, Wendy Ogden
Designer: Nick Shearn
Illustrations: Katie Jardine, Ian Moule, Carlie Jennings, Tony Wynn, Lori Head, Hilda Knight

A catalogue record for this book is available from the British Library
Library of Congress Control Number 2006900196

ISBN13 978-1-4129-1961-6
ISBN10 1-4129-1961-4 (pbk)

Printed on paper from sustainable resources
Printed in Great Britain by The Cromwell Press Ltd, Trowbridge, Wiltshire

The CD-ROM contains PDF files, labelled 'Worksheets.pdf' which consists of the stories and worksheets for each unit in this resource. You will need Acrobat Reader version 3 or higher to view and print these resources.

The documents are set up to print to A4 but you can enlarge them to A3 by increasing the output percentage at the point of printing using the page set-up settings for your printer.

Contents

The *Promoting Children's Resilience and Wellbeing* series were originally published in Australia as the Values for Life series of books, and when we saw them we felt they would provide valuable additions to our range of books on emotional literacy. One of the attractions was that the four books provided a coherent programme from early years through to 12.

Book 1: *Learning to be Honest, Kind and Friendly* (Age range: 5 to 7)

Book 2: *Learning to be Confident, Determined and Caring* (Age range: 5 to 7)

Book 3: *Developing Consideration, Respect and Tolerance* (Age range: 7 to 9)

Book 4: *Enhancing Courage, Respect and Assertiveness* (Age range: 9 to 12)

In Australia the term 'emotional resilience' is more widely used than in the UK, though the term is increasingly current here. Resilience is the ability to recover from adversity or difficult situations or circumstances. Fuller (2001) suggests that life events are 'contagious'. Life events, both positive and negative, establish chains of behaviour. If children are faced with negative events their interpretation of these events will influence how they cope. If they don't have resilience he is likely to react in a negative way.

An example of a negative or risk chain would be:

a child who grows up in violent circumstances and learns to distrust others, enters school and interprets the intention of others as hostile. The child then acts warily or aggressively towards peers and develops peer relationship problems…

An example of a positive or protective chain would be:

a child who grows up in violent circumstances but learns, on entry to school, that there is a trustworthy adult who can be relied on to assist in the resolution of peer relationship difficulties. The child's positive attempts to interact with others are acknowledged. The child begins to feel accepted, mixes more appropriately with peers and develops a diversity of friendships. (Fuller, 2001)

The work of Goleman (1995) indicates that the promotion of protective factors in school life is not only predictive of academic success but even more importantly for positive adult life outcomes.

The idea of positive factors that promote resilience has been supported by research (Resnick, Harris and Blum, 1993; Fuller, McGraw and Goodyear, 1998). The main factors appear to be:

▸ family connectedness

▸ peer connectedness

▸ fitting in at school.

Two of these can be directly influenced by school life, creating positive experiences that are 'contagious'.

Resilience seems to depend largely on this sense of belonging. Once one belongs, empathy can develop and empathy builds group cohesion where moral actions such as honesty, altruism and caring emerge developmentally as the child matures.

This idea of resilience can be seen to be important in all areas of school life, as quoted in Fuller (2001):

When schools promote belonging and ensure high levels of involvement between staff and students, bullying is reduced.

(Citing the work of Olweus, 1995; Rigby 1996.)

This series, with its progressive programme, allows the opportunity for young people to explore:

- consideration
- honesty
- responsibility
- confidence
- courage
- caring
- friendliness
- kindness
- tolerance
- respect
- determination
- assertiveness.

As children mature the level that these can be explored becomes deeper; their reasoning and morality becomes more sophisticated with age and this type of programme can assist in their 'connectedness'. Our increasing awareness of the concept of 'Citizenship' should recognise elements such as empathy, moral reasoning and moral behaviour.

Current UK initiatives

The Healthy Schools Programme identifies emotional health and wellbeing (including bullying) as one of the areas schools have to develop and are required to produce evidence that they have met the necessary criteria. The Healthy Schools Programme, of course, is not a separate entity divorced from all other aspects of school development. The statutory components of PSHE and Citizenship for primary schools can be linked to the concept of emotional health and wellbeing and, we would also argue, emotional resilience.

The 12 domains covered in this programme fit the four components of PSHE and Citizenship at Key Stage 1 and 2:

1. Developing confidence and responsibility and making the most of their abilities.

2. Preparing to play an active role as citizens.

3. Developing a healthy, safer lifestyle.

4. Developing good relationships and respecting the difference between people.

The introduction of developing children's social, emotional and behavioural skills (SEBS) also highlights the importance of the type of material presented in this book.

- Emotional and social competence have been shown to be more influential than cognitive abilities for personal, career and scholastic success.

- Programmes that teach social and emotional competences have been shown to result in a wide range of educational gains.

- Work and workplace increasingly focus on social and emotional competences with increased emphasis on teamwork, communication, management skills etc. (DfES, 2003)

Though resilience is not mentioned directly, SEBS clearly identifies the earlier point about the 'contagious' effects of life events.

> Research is bringing home the wide extent of various types of neglect and abuse. This is being exacerbated by the breakdown of extended family and communities which reduces support for the nuclear family, and the higher rates of divorce and subsequent one-parent families. This has led to a shake-up in belief that we can leave children's emotional and social development to parents... so schools have to provide the emotional and social guidance that some pupils currently lack. (DfES, 2003)

However, helping young people develop emotional resilience isn't just for young people from disturbed or disturbing backgrounds. School life and home life can be stressful for all young people, and with the growing awareness of the importance of emotional literacy, the *Promoting Children's Resilience and Wellbeing* series will be an ideal programme to support a key element, emotional resilience.

George Robinson and Barbara Maines

The *Promoting Children's Resilience and Wellbeing* series is a whole–school, values based programme. It is designed to assist in the creation of wellbeing and resilience in young students by introducing them to a range of values and behaviours that, when practised, can promote social and emotional health.

The programme, stories and activities are also designed to enhance the development of a positive learning environment and literacy skills.

Learning to be Confident, Determined and Caring is suitable for 5 to 7 year olds. Each story introduces young students to the language and associated behaviours of six important values relevant to the development of social and emotional health of children in school settings:

1. Confidence

2. Respect

3. Courage

4. Determination

5. Caring

6. Assertiveness.

This series is designed to assist in the development of wellbeing and resilience in young students.

The values in the stories complement the following four areas:

1. Social, emotional and behavioural skills

2. Creation of supportive learning environments

3. Development of language acquisition

4. Development of wellbeing and resilience in young students.

Social, Emotional and Behavioural Skills

These stories introduce students, in a formal way, to the 'language' of prosocial values and behaviours that assist in promoting social and emotional wellbeing. Each story focuses upon identifiable values and behaviours that fit the requirements of the PSHE and Citizenship curriculum for children aged 5 to 12.

Creating Supportive Learning Environments

Students are more willing to participate in learning environments if they feel safe and secure in the classroom and have a sense of connectedness or bonding with their teachers and peers. A secure and supportive learning environment optimises the students' willingness to take risks.

The *Promoting Children's Resilience and Wellbeing* programme introduces students to the values and behaviours that assist in promoting a sense of safety, security, and social and emotional wellbeing in school settings. When practised, these values reinforce the development of three essential elements in the construction and maintenance of effective teaching and learning environments:

1. A sense of safety and security.

2. A sense of belonging.

3. A sense of cooperation and harmony.

Development of Language Acquisition

The stories in the *Promoting Children's Resilience and Wellbeing* programme introduce young students to the 'language' of prosocial values and behaviours. The stories are designed to expand knowledge and understanding of many of the values and behaviours that assist in developing wellbeing, and to build language skills via listening, reading, discussion and related activities.

Development of Wellbeing and Resilience

The *Promoting Children's Resilience and Wellbeing* programme assists students in creating a better understanding of some of the related values and behaviours that help to promote social and emotional wellbeing and resilience. (See the chart on pages 3 and 4 for links.)

The stories are designed to support the development of resilience, focusing on three key areas:

1. **Self-appreciation**
    Introducing concepts of self-worth, self-efficacy, problem-solving skills, responsibility, courage to try new things, patience, acknowledging past successes and excellence.

2. **Social competence**
    Introducing concepts of friendliness, helpfulness, caring, empathy, flexibility, sense of humour, assertiveness, generosity, tolerance, courtesy, respect, fairness, cleanliness, cooperation, honesty, reliability, stress and anxiety management skills and forgiveness.

3. **Sense of optimistic future**
    Introducing concepts such as the importance of having goals, positive expectations, enthusiasm, determination, perseverance, self-discipline, optimism and organisational skills.

Guidelines for Value, Story and Resilience Links

These illustrate the links between the curriculum, value, story, resilience and wellbeing promoting factors.

VALUE	TITLE	SELF-APPRECIATION	SOCIAL COMPETENCE	SENSE OF OPTIMISTIC FUTURE	LINKS BETWEEN STORY, WELLBEING AND RESILIENCE
CONFIDENCE	At School	●		●	Recognition of the feeling that confidence brings and a sense of achievement.
CONFIDENCE	The Rollerblader	●		●	Recognition that confidence is enhanced with the mastering of a skill
CONFIDENCE	Frozen Statues	●	●	●	Recognition that social competence and confidence develops with participation.
CONFIDENCE	The Beach	●		●	Recognition of things done with confidence and having a sense of fun.
RESPECT	Did You Ask?	●	●	●	Respecting the belongings of self and others. Developing good verbal communication. Maintaining future positive relationships.
RESPECT	Mr Khatum's Roses		●	●	Building positive relationships with neighbours, so they can go there in the future. Demonstrating respect for gardens.
RESPECT	Kate's In The Shower	●	●	●	Respecting individual privacy. Using cooperation to overcome problems. Maintaining positive relationships.
RESPECT	Our School Grounds	●		●	Taking responsibility for the school grounds. Wanting a pleasant environment for future play.
COURAGE	The Surprise	●	●	●	Recognising the need for courage in some social situations.
COURAGE	The Diving Board	●		●	Recognising that sometimes, to try a new skill, we need to show courage.
COURAGE	The Holiday	●		●	Recognising that sometimes things that are unpleasant are necessary, and that we may need courage to complete an unpleasant task or requirement.
COURAGE	The Chairlift	●		●	Demonstrating courage by a willingness to participate in new experiences.

Guidelines for Value, Story and Resilience Links

VALUE	TITLE	SELF-APPRECIATION	SOCIAL COMPETENCE	SENSE OF OPTIMISTIC FUTURE	LINKS BETWEEN STORY, WELLBEING AND RESILIENCE
DETERMINATION	Keep On Trying	●		●	Developing and appreciating the skill of tying shoelaces, so that in the future no help is needed.
	Just A Bit More	●		●	Overcoming the problem of eating vegetables. Knowing what is wanted afterwards. Using determination to achieve an end.
	Let's Go Riding	●		●	Developing the skill of bike riding. Wanting to ride a bike in the future. Setting a goal.
	Mum's Birthday	●	●		Developing the skill of cake making. Recognising special events in other's lives.
CARING	Caring For Young Ones	●	●	●	The importance of caring for self and others. Expectations of being able to care in relationships.
	My Dad's A Nurse	●	●	●	Recognition of the skill of caring professions. Using humour to help others feel better. Future employment in caring industries.
	Grandpa's Medals	●		●	Recognition of Grandpa's achievements. Personal responsibility for the care of medals.
	The Chicken	●		●	Being willing to take care of a sick animal. Knowing that how we care for something may affect its future. Being optimistic of a positive future.
ASSERTIVENESS	Let's Go In Here	●	●	●	Developing the skill of assertiveness. Being able to say, 'No,' to friends. Knowing how to use assertiveness in the future.
	What I Do Well	●	●		Being able to recognise your own skills, and speaking in an assertive manner to a group.
	Thiery's Toys	●	●	●	Recognising the importance of appreciating others and their belongings. Saying, 'No,' so the toys are in good condition for future play.
	The Blue Pencil	●	●	●	Solving a problem. Acting in a cooperative, assertive and friendly way. Having coloured pencils for all to use.

To use the programme the facilitator will:

▶ Choose a prosocial value as a focus.

▶ Print or photocopy the relevant story for your students. Each story has two accompanying activity sheets.

▶ Read and discuss the story with the students identifying the specific prosocial values. This will assist students in building a language of prosocial values and behaviours.

▶ Ask the students to paste the story into a scrapbook. The scrapbook can be taken home and read with the family.

Promoting Children's Resilience and Wellbeing

The Programme

1. Confidence

2. Respect

3. Courage

4. Determination

5. Caring

6. Assertiveness

1

I can do lots of things at school with confidence.

2

I can write my name with confidence.

3

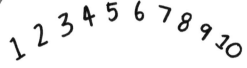

I can count to ten with confidence.

4

I can build a sandcastle with confidence.

5

I can tie my shoelaces with confidence.

6

I can sing a song with confidence.

7

I can paint a picture of a dog with confidence...

8

and I can smile with confidence.

Activity 1

In the space below, draw and label things that you can do at school with confidence.

~~~
**Things I can do with confidence:**
~~~

Activity 2

Colour in the outlined word:

I can count to ten with

confidence

Match the words and numbers below.

1.
2.
3.
4.
5.
6.
7.
8.
9.
10.

four   three

ten

six   nine   two

eight   seven

five   one

On the back of the sheet, write and draw about something that you can do at home with confidence.

1

For my birthday, I was given a pair of rollerblades, knee and elbow pads and a helmet. Mum was going to help me to rollerblade.

2

After school, I sat on the driveway and put on my rollerblades. Mum helped me stand up. I felt very wobbly.

3

I held on to Mum's hands tightly. She showed me how to move my feet, legs and arms. 'I can do that,' I thought.

4

I rolled forward. Mum let go of my hands. I rolled into the fence. I pushed one foot at a time: left, right, left. I let go of the fence.

5

I was moving slowly along the footpath. I wobbled and fell over. 'Try again,' said Mum. I stood up, rubbed my knee and kept going.

6

and around the corner. Soon, I was rollerblading with confidence.

7

Mum was clapping as I rollerbladed up to her.

I felt very proud of myself.

Activity 1

In the space below, draw and write about something that you do with confidence at school, and something you do with confidence at home.

~~~
School
~~~

~~~
Home
~~~

Activity 2

The rollerblader practised a lot before she could rollerblade with confidence.

She wore special equipment to help keep her safe.

Draw the equipment to match the correct name.

Helmet

Knee pads

Elbow pads

Rollerblades

Explain on the lines below how wearing safety equipment can help you to feel more confident when you try something new.

On the back of the sheet, list three activities which may require safety equipment to help you feel safer and more confident.

1

Tania invited me to her birthday party.

I didn't know anyone who was going.

'Just relax and be friendly,' Mum said.

2

When I arrived, I gave Tania her present.

She asked me to join in a game.

I said I'd watch for a while.

3

They were playing frozen statues. I knew how to play.

I decided to join in. The more I played frozen statues, the more confident I became.

4

We had lots of fun.

At the end of the party, I said thank you to Tania.

I was glad I had used my confidence that day.

Activity 1

List five tips you would give to a nervous person to help build their confidence at a party (e.g. smile, ask someone a question).

1. _____

2. _____

3. _____

4. _____

5. _____

Activity 2

Often, the more we practise something the better we become at it and the more confident we feel.

In the space below, write and draw about a time this has happened to you.

1

I go to the beach with my family and have a great time.

2

I jump over waves with confidence.

3

I build sandcastles with confidence.

4

I walk along the beach and look at shells.

5

I scare some crabs. They hold up their pincers at me with confidence.

6

I fly my kite with confidence.

7

At the end of the day, I watch the birds fly high in the sky with confidence.

I always have a lot of fun at the beach.

Activity 1

Cut and paste the words from the bottom of the page to complete the sentences.

A spider builds a _____ with confidence.

A bird builds a _____ with confidence.

A caterpillar makes a _____ with confidence.

A bee makes _____ with confidence.

I can make a _____ with confidence.

✂ ···

| honeycomb | sandcastle | cocoon | web | nest |

Activity 2

In the blank photo space below, draw a picture of yourself doing something with confidence.

This is a picture of me full of confidence:

On the lines below, write about your picture and how 'confidence' feels to you.

Respect

1

Tom picked up Dad's hammer. Mum said, 'Did you ask?'

2

'Dad, please may I use your hammer?' asked Tom.

'Yes,' said Dad.

3

Tom picked up Ann's skateboard. Mum said, 'Did you ask?'

4

'Ann, please may I ride your skateboard?' asked Tom.

'Yes,' said Ann.

5

Mum says it shows respect to ask before you use someone else's things.

6

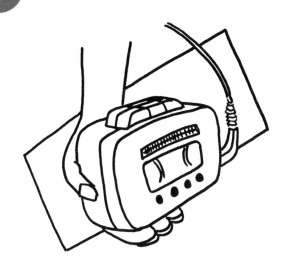

Mum picked up Tom's Walkman.

7

'May I, Tom?' asked Mum.

'Yes,' said Tom, 'and thank you for asking first.'

Activity 1

Draw a picture of each of the items you wish to borrow and who, from the story, you would ask.

May I ride your skateboard, please?

May I use your hammer, please?

May I use your Walkman, please?

Activity 2

Colour in the outlined word.

It shows respect to ask before you use things that belong to others.

Draw and label four things that you have asked someone if you could use.

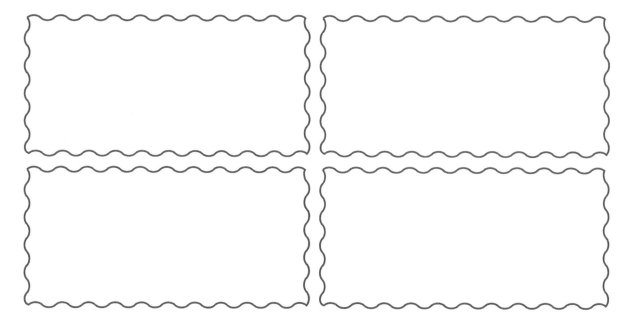

1

I live next door to Mr Khatum.

Mr Khatum grows beautiful roses in his garden.

Sometimes, when my brother and I play ball, it goes over the fence and into Mr Khatum's yard.

2

Mr Khatum doesn't mind if we come into his yard and get our ball, as long as we are careful and don't damage his roses.

3

Mum says it's important to respect other people's gardens.

Once, I had to use a rake to get my ball out of Mr Khatum's rose garden, so I wouldn't be prickled.

4

I think Mr Khatum's roses are pretty, but their prickles aren't.

I'm glad we don't have roses in our garden.

5

Yesterday, it was Mum's birthday.

Guess what Mr Khatum gave Mum?

6

A rose to start her own rose garden.

Activity 1

Mr Khatum grows roses in his garden.
Colour them in.

One red rose, two pink roses and three
yellow roses.

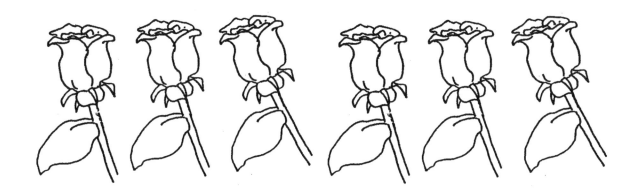

Draw two prickles on each rose.

How many prickles altogether? _____

How many leaves altogether? _____

Count the roses.

🌹🌹🌹 + 🌹🌹🌹 = _____

🌹🌹 + 🌹🌹🌹 = _____

On the back of this sheet, draw and name your own rose.

Activity 2

What tool was used to get the ball safely from Mr Khatum's garden?

— __ __ __ __

Colour in the outlined words and draw lines to the correct picture.

Ladder

Rope

Rake

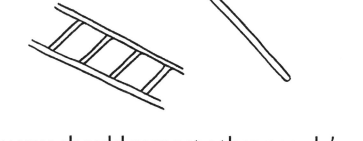

Write and draw why you should respect other people's gardens.

1

My big sister, Kate, takes a long time in the bathroom.

2

If I go into the bathroom, Kate screams, 'I'm not finished yet! You will have to wait.'

3

Sometimes, I feel like I'm waiting forever just to use the bathroom.

4

Once, when Kate was taking too long under the shower, I quietly opened the door and let Harold, my pet mouse, in.

5

Kate screamed! That hurried her up! Mum said that wasn't a very kind thing to do to my sister or the mouse.

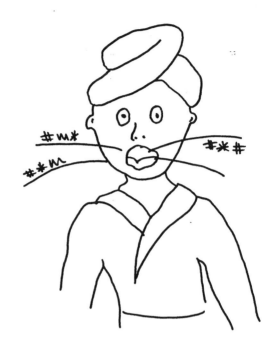

6

Mum said I needed to learn to respect Kate's privacy, and that Kate needed to hurry up in the shower.

7

We made a family rule.

No more than five minutes under the shower.

Now, I knock on the door when Kate has been more than five minutes under the shower.

8

If that doesn't hurry Kate up, I can always use my secret weapon, Harold!

Activity 1

What do you think Mum meant when she said, 'I needed to learn to respect Kate's privacy'?

Make a list of three bathroom rules you have in your home.

1.

2.

3.

Activity 2

Write what you do if someone in your family is taking too long under the shower.

Mark the times on the clocks below.

9.15

3.30

8.00

12.30

1

At our school, we have beautiful trees and gardens.

We respect the school grounds and take good care of the garden.

2

Each week, Mr Green and a group of children work in the garden. They wear special hats.

3

They unlock the garden shed and take out spades, wheelbarrows, weeding forks and gardening gloves.

4

Some days, they weed the gardens and put fertiliser on the plants to help them grow. Some days, they plant seeds and bulbs in the garden beds.

5

On very hot days, they water the trees. Mr Green likes to be cooled down on those days too.

6

We respect and care for our school grounds. They are a great place to play.

Activity 1

Fill in the missing words.

They wear special h _ _ _.
They use wheelbarrows and s _ _ _ _ _ .
They w _ _ _ the garden.
They plant s _ _ _ _ .
They w _ _ _ _ the trees.

On the back of this sheet, design the perfect school grounds for children to play in. Remember the garden!

Activity 2

List three things you do that show you respect your school grounds.

1.

2.

3.

Design a sign that asks people to respect your school grounds.

1

It was my birthday. My school friends said they had a surprise for me inside the classroom.

2

My friends said I needed to close my eyes tightly and come with them.

3

They led me carefully along the corridor. I felt a bit nervous, but I used courage and kept going.

4

My friends led me into our classroom. 'Surprise!' they yelled. 'Open your eyes.' I did, and there in front of me was a big cake with candles on it. 'Happy Birthday!' they all said.

Activity 1

Draw a picture of a surprise party for your teacher in your classroom.

Remember to draw the decorations.

Activity 2

Draw a picture or write about a time when you showed courage.

1

I went with my friends to the pool. There was a high diving board at the pool.

2

All of my friends could jump off the diving board. I thought, if they can do it, so can I.

3

I climbed halfway up. I looked down. I felt scared.

4

I climbed to the top. I looked down. I felt scared.

5

I held my nose. I closed my eyes. I jumped. Splash!

6

My friends clapped and cheered! 'That was fun!' I called out.

7

I can use my courage any time that I feel a bit scared.

Activity 1

Colour in the outlined words.

The boy showed his

courage

to jump off the board.

You can show your

courage

whenever you need to.

On the back of this sheet, design a medal that you would give someone for their courage.

Activity 2

Find these words in this word search.

courage	high	scared
climbed	jump	diving
friends	board	pool
splash	cheered	

k	j	d	u	n	l	k	d	i	u	f	a	j	p	g	j	k
a	k	i	c	o	u	r	a	g	e	l	o	m	d	f	d	j
j	u	m	p	j	d	i	n	v	l	k	j	i	s	r	i	i
j	k	o	a	m	d	p	s	h	b	k	k	c	c	i	o	n
a	d	d	i	v	i	n	g	j	o	j	i	h	h	e	n	a
i	i	a	p	e	i	n	m	g	a	a	o	e	e	n	a	l
j	n	s	i	p	o	o	l	w	r	i	n	e	e	d	n	d
n	s	c	a	k	s	k	q	r	d	n	k	r	r	s	l	i
d	l	a	n	a	p	i	o	s	s	d	a	e	e	k	i	n
l	d	r	s	i	l	n	p	t	h	k	i	d	d	l	d	a
n	i	e	l	n	a	d	d	i	v	j	u	k	k	p	n	d
k	a	d	i	d	s	c	l	i	m	b	e	d	k	j	i	n
l	e	l	d	l	h	k	d	i	n	l	k	j	i	h	l	k
k	p	k	n	s	j	h	w	l	h	i	g	h	k	d	i	n

1

Mum and Dad were taking us overseas for a holiday.

'We will go on a big plane,' said Mum. 'We will visit other countries,' said Mum.

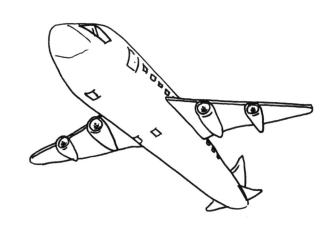

2

'We will need to go to the doctor first,' said Mum.

'Yes, we will need to have an injection before we go,' said Dad.

'An injection!' I thought.

3

The holiday sounded great, but the injection didn't.

The plane sounded great, but the injection didn't.

4

We all went to the doctor. Mum had her injection first. It didn't hurt Mum. Dad was next. It didn't hurt Dad. I was next.

5

I thought, if they can do it, so can I. I sat on the chair.

I used my courage. I was brave.

6

The doctor made me laugh then said I could go. I'd already had the injection! At last, I was ready for our overseas holiday.

Activity 1

In the story, the family was going overseas.

The girl wasn't scared about the flight, but she needed her courage to have what?

Circle the correct answer.

She needed her courage to have an

_____.

Fill in the missing letters.

I will try to show

_ _ _ _ _ _ _ _ .

Activity 2

Answer the clues to solve this crossword.

DOWN

1. Name of the story.
2. What the girl needed to use in the story.

ACROSS

3. Not underseas.
4. What the girl needed courage for.
5. Flies through the sky.
6. Not scared.

COURAGE

PLANE

OVERSEAS

HOLIDAY

BRAVE

INJECTION

1

'Let's all go skiing,' said Dad.

'That sounds like fun,' we all said.

2

I was looking forward to skiing.

But I wasn't looking forward to the chairlift.

'Don't worry,' said Dad, 'I will be right beside you.'

3

We arrived at the mountain. I looked up at the chairlift.

'Don't worry,' said Dad, 'I will be right beside you.'

4

We stood beside the chairlift. 'Don't worry,' said Dad,

'I will be right beside you.' I thought, 'I will use my courage to go on the chairlift.'

5

Dad and I sat on the chairlift.

'Don't worry,' said Dad, 'I am right beside you.'

6

'Don't worry, Dad. This is fun,' I said.

I can use my courage any time I feel a bit scared.

Activity 1

Draw a picture of yourself on a chairlift and draw other things you might see at the snowfields.

Write about a time that you used courage to achieve something.

Activity 2

Use the clues to solve the crossword below.

DOWN

1. You can do this on a snowfield.
2. Colour of snow.
3. The boy used his courage to go on this.
4. Have a good time.

ACROSS

1. White and cold.
5. What does the boy show in the story?

COURAGE

CHAIRLIFT

SKIING

WHITE

ENJOY

SNOW

Determination

1

On Monday, I tried to tie my shoelaces.

2

'Keep on trying,' said Mum.

3

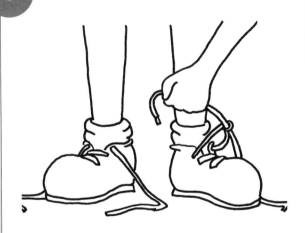

On Tuesday, I tried to tie my shoelaces.
'Keep on trying,' said Mum.

4

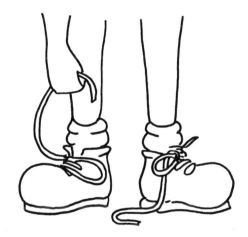

On Wednesday, I tried to tie my shoelaces.

'Keep on trying,' said Mum.

5

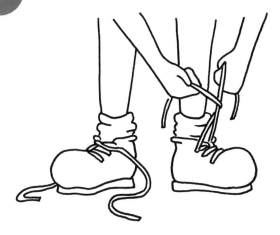

On Thursday, I tried to tie my shoelaces.

'Keep on trying,' said Mum.

6

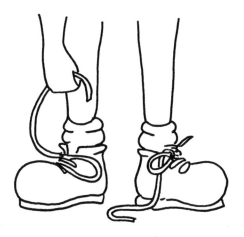

On Friday, I was really determined to tie my shoelaces.

7

'Keep on trying,' said Mum.

8

'Yes, I did it!'

'Well done. I knew you could do it,' said Mum.

Activity 1

Draw round the boots and colour them in.
Draw the laces tied in a bow.

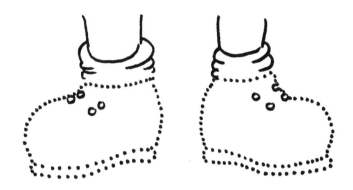

Colour in the outlined words.

Each day, Mum said,

'Keep on trying.'

Copy the sentence on the line below.

On Friday, I tied my shoelaces.

_____

_____

Activity 2

Match the shoes.

Colour the shoes, then cut them out and paste the matching shoes onto the blank squares.

Red runners

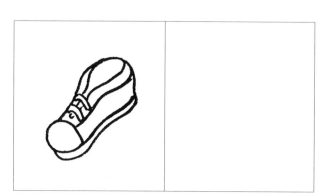

Yellow boots

Green slippers

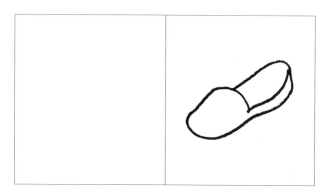

Blue flip-flops

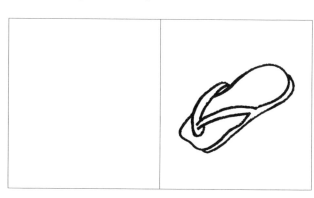

1

Mum made a chocolate pudding and custard for dessert: my favourite!

2

Mum said I could have some pudding if I ate all my vegetables first. 'I don't like vegetables!' I said. But I was determined to have dessert.

3

I walked over to the pantry and found the tomato sauce. I covered all of the vegetables with tomato sauce so I couldn't taste them as much.

4

I ate the squashy pumpkin. Yuk! Then the peas and beans. Yuk! 'Just a bit more,' I said to myself. 'Then I can have dessert.'

5

I covered the brussels sprouts with lots of tomato sauce. I chewed them quickly so I couldn't taste them as much. Yuk!

6

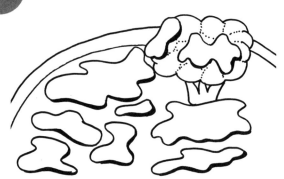

'Just a bit more,' I said to myself. 'Then I can have dessert.' Only the cauliflower to eat.

7

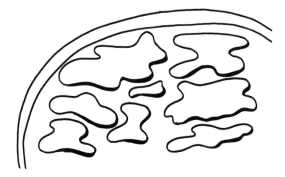

I mixed the cauliflower with the sauce. I held my nose and swallowed quickly. Hooray! I've finally done it! I've eaten all the vegetables on the plate.

8

Now I can have my chocolate pudding and custard. Yum!

Activity 1

Colour in the outlined sentence below.

I like chocolate pudding.

Colour the pudding.

Draw custard on the top of the pudding.

Draw a line to match the words to the pictures. Colour in.

cauliflower

carrots

green beans

peas

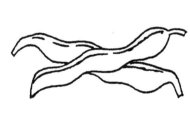

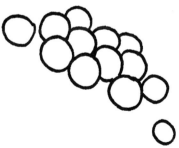

Activity 2

How many pumpkins are there?

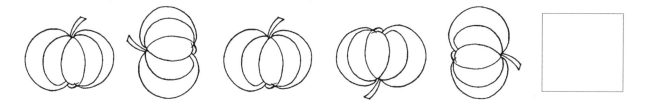

Draw three orange pumpkins.   Draw four green beans.

Draw six fat carrots.   Draw the other half of the plate so that both sides look the same.

1

Amy was going camping at the weekend with her family and some friends.

2

Amy loved camping, but she had a problem that she was worried about.

3

All of Amy's friends could ride bikes, but she couldn't.

4

Amy had never learned to ride a bike before.

5

At the camp site, there were bikes of all sizes and colours.

6

Big bikes, small bikes, pink bikes, BMX bikes and bikes with trainer wheels.

7

Amy watched the children having fun riding their bikes.

8

She was determined to learn to ride a bike that weekend.

9

Amy's sister held the bike steady while Amy got on.

10

Amy's mum held the back of the bike and ran behind.

11

Amy pedalled faster and faster. She wobbled a bit.

12

She pedalled faster. Amy's mum let go Lof the bike.

13

'Look at me!' yelled Amy happily!

14

'I'm riding on my own!'

15

Everyone cheered!

Activity 1

Colour in the outlined word.

Amy was determined to learn to ride a bike.

Draw the bikes that were at the campsite.

A small bike	A pink bike
A BMX bike	A bike with trainer wheels

How many wheels altogether? _____

Activity 2

Label the parts of Amy's bike.

seat	**pedals**
handle bars	**tyres**
spokes	**chain**

Draw Amy riding on the bike, then colour it in.

1

It was Mum's birthday. I was determined to make her favourite cake.

2

A chocolate cake! Yum!

3

I found the chocolate biscuits in the pantry. I took the cream out of the fridge.

4

I used the beater to whip the cream until it was thick.

5

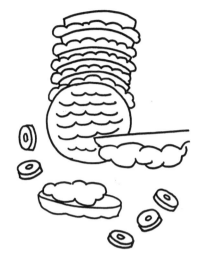

I put cream between the biscuits. I joined them all together to make a cake.

6

I covered the outside of the cake with thick cream, and decorated it with sweets and candles.

7

Mum said it was the best birthday cake that she'd ever had.

Activity 1

Put the sentences in the correct order.

☐ I used the beater to whip the cream.

☐ I decorated the cake with sweets and candles.

☐ I was determined to make Mum a cake.

☐ I found the chocolate biscuits in the pantry.

☐ I put cream between the biscuits.

Draw Mum's birthday cake below.

Activity 2

Below are six birthday cakes.

Draw five candles on each cake.

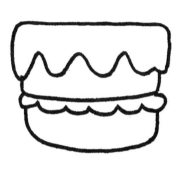

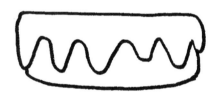

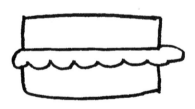

How many candles altogether?   _____

How many candles on three cakes?   _____

How many candles on five cakes?   _____

1

The dog cares for her puppy.

2

The sheep cares for her lamb.

3

The hen cares for her chickens.

4

The cat cares for her kitten.

5

The horse cares for her foal.

6

And Mum and Dad...

7

...care for me.

Activity 1

Help the kitten find its way to the cat.

Colour in the outlined sentence below.

The cat is caring for the kittens.

On the back of this sheet, draw a cat with three kittens.

Activity 2

Colour in the animals, then cut out and paste to match the sentences

The cat cares for its

The dog cares for its

The sheep cares for its

The hen cares for its

| chick | puppy | kitten | lamb |

1

My dad's a nurse. He works at a big hospital.

2

Dad wears a special uniform and a name badge with his photo on it.

3

Dad takes people's temperature and changes bandages.

He helps sick people to the bathroom.

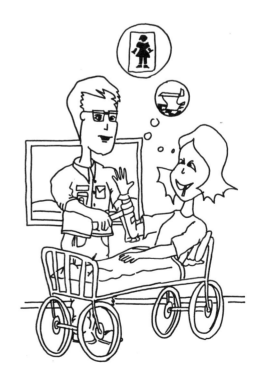

4

Dad wheels people to X-ray to see if they have a broken bone. He tells them jokes and funny stories.

5

If I ever go to hospital, I hope I have a nurse just like my dad to care for me.

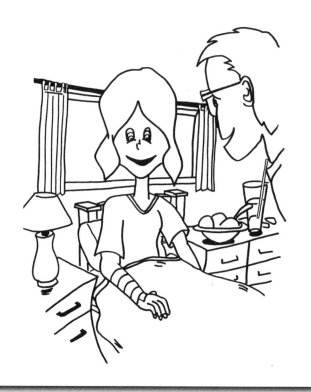

Activity 1

A nurse takes your temperature.

Show the temperatures on the thermometers below.

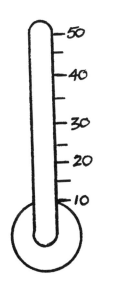

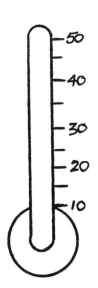

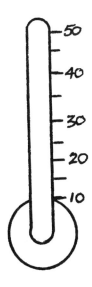

Show 25°　　　　**Show 35°**　　　　**Show 40°**

Add the length of the bandages.

10cm　+　20cm　= _____

5cm　+　10cm　= _____

15cm　+　10cm　= _____

9cm　+　9cm　= _____

Activity 2

A nurse cares for sick people.

Use the clues to solve the crossword below.

DOWN

1. Where you go when you are sick.
2. What you wrap around a broken bone.
5. Who looks after you in hospital?

ACROSS

2. What do you lie on in hospital?
3. What are you given to feel better?
4. You receive lots of this in hospital.
6. What is used to see inside the body?

NURSE
BANDAGE
HOSPITAL
BED
MEDICINE
CARING
X-RAY

1

It was Remembrance Day. Nana showed me some of Grandpa's medals.

Grandpa had died a long time ago.

2

His medals were very special to Nana.

Nana said I could take Grandpa's medals to school and show the class.

3

I promised Nana I would take good care of Grandpa's medals. They were very special to me too.

4

I told my class about Grandpa and showed his medals with pride. The next day, I gave them safely back to Nana.

5

Nana thanked me for taking such good care of Grandpa's medals.

Then she gave me a big hug.

Activity 1

Colour in the outlined words and fill in the missing word.

Nana is caring.

I took care of Grandpa's medals.

Nana cares for me.

I _ _ _ _ for Nana.

On the back of this sheet, draw a picture of you caring for someone.

Activity 2

Join the dots then colour in.

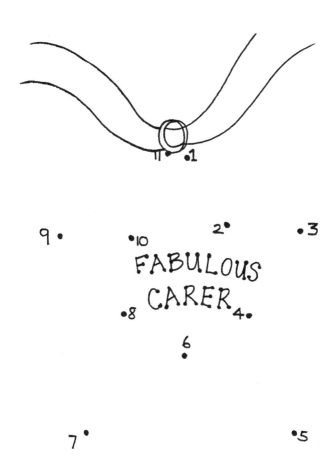

Write about some things that you are good at caring for.

I am good at caring for:

1

Our hen had been sitting on her eggs for days and days.

At last, the chicks hatched. The chicks were fluffy and noisy.

2

One of the chicks looked weak and very sick.

Dad and I put the sick chick in a box and took it to see the vet.

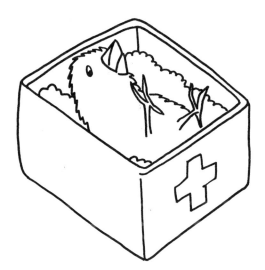

3

The vet gave the chick some special medicine, and told us how to care for the sick chick.

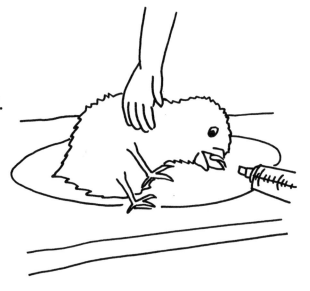

4

I gave the chick medicine for five days. I had to keep the chick safe and warm too.

5

Soon the chick was well again. Hooray! Hooray!

We put the chick back with its family. The mother hen was so happy to have her chick home, safe and well again.

6

Dad said I had cared for the chick very well.

Activity 1

Read the sentences below and draw the matching picture in each box.

1	2
3	4

1. The egg has been laid.
2. The egg begins to crack.
3. The chick pecks its way out of the egg.
4. The chick is standing up.

On the back of this sheet, make a list of some of the things you would need to take good care of a chick.

Activity 2

Find some words about chickens in this word search.

grain	rooster	sunshine	fluffy
water	egg	henhouse	beak
hen	nest	yellow	feather

R	H	E	N	E	A	D	B	E	A	K	A
O	R	W	E	G	K	F	L	U	F	F	Y
O	S	A	G	G	R	A	I	N	E	L	E
S	T	T	P	A	K	W	U	N	A	M	L
T	H	E	N	H	O	U	S	E	T	K	L
E	O	R	Q	L	C	G	S	S	H	R	O
R	U	N	Z	E	N	J	F	T	E	S	W
M	S	U	N	S	H	I	N	E	R	V	K

On the back of this sheet, draw a chicken and label these parts.

Eyes **Beak** **Legs** **Wings**

Assertiveness

1

'Let's go in here,'
said Simon.

'No,' I said
assertively.

2

'Let's go in here,' said
Simon. 'No,' I said
assertively.

3

'Let's go up here,' said
Simon. 'No,' I said
assertively.

4

'Let's go down here,' said Simon. 'No,' I said assertively.

5

'Let's go in here,' said Simon.

'Great!' I said with a smile.

Assertiveness – Let's Go In Here

Activity 1

Help the boys find their way to the park.

List three places that you like to play with your friends.

1.

2.

3.

Activity 2

Draw about a time you had to stand up for yourself and be assertive.

Write down what is the best thing about you.

1

Today at school, I told my class what I can do well.

2

'I can ride my bike really well,' I said assertively.

3

'I can make my own lunch,' I said assertively.

4

'I can tie my shoelaces without any help,' I said assertively.

5

'I can feed the cat and dog without making a mess,' I said assertively.

6

'I can water the vegetable garden without getting wet,' I said assertively.

7

And sometimes...

I can lick the chocolate cake mixing bowl very clean.

Activity 1

In the boxes below, draw some of the things you can do well.

My favourite thing to do is:

Colour in the outlined sentence below.

I can do it.

Activity 2

Colour in the outlined words, then fill in the missing word.

'I can tie my shoelaces,'
I said assertively.

'I can ride my bike,'
I said assertively.

'I can make my lunch,' I said _ _ _ _ _ _ _ _ _ _ _ _ _ _.

1

'Thiery!' Mum called.

'Is this your puzzle all over the floor?'

2

Thiery and I looked at each other. 'Whoops,' we said.

3

My brother Thiery is not very old, but he looks after his toys very well.

4

He puts his toys away each day before he goes to school.

5

One day, Becky came to play. She tried to break Thiery's toys.

'Stop,' I said assertively. 'I will not let you break Thiery's toys.'

6

Adam came over to play. He tried to break one of Thiery's toys. 'Stop,' I said assertively. 'I will not let you break Thiery's toys.'

7

When Thiery came home from school, he hugged me.

8

'Thank you for looking after my toys,' Thiery said.

Activity 1

If a friend was being rough with your favourite toy, what would you say to them to make them play with your toy more gently?

Design a sign for your bedroom that lets others know how you would like them to treat your toys.

Activity 2

Thiery looked after his toys very well.

Draw your favourite toy and write a sentence about how you care for it.

1

This is our classroom.

On each table is a tin of coloured pencils.

2

We all share the coloured pencils, except my friend Jack.

3

Jack doesn't share the pencils very well, especially the blue one.

4

One day, Jack wasn't sharing the blue pencil.

We all needed to use the blue pencil. We had a meeting.

5

We needed to be assertive with Jack. We made up a rule.

Each person could use a colour for only a short time.

Then it went back in the tin for others to use.

6

Now Jack's drawings are very colourful, and we all have a turn at using the blue pencil.

Activity 1

Each packet of pencils contains 10 pencils.

How many pencils are there altogether?

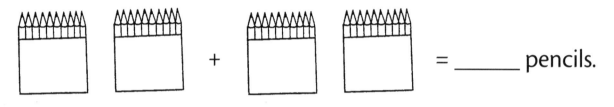

= _____ pencils.

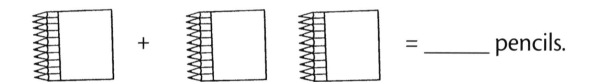

= _____ pencils.

= _____ pencils.

List 3 things that you share with others in your class.

1.

2.

3.

On the back of the sheet, write about a time you needed to be assertive in your class.

Activity 2

The students in the story made a group rule about the use of the coloured pencils.

They were assertive.

In the space below, write about another problem the children in your class may have had and how you would solve it assertively.

Benard, B. (1995) *Fostering Resiliency in Kids: Protective Factors in the Family, School and Community*, Western Centre for Drug Free Schools and Communities, Portland, Oregon.

Cahill, H. (1999) 'Why a 'Whole School' Approach to Enhancing Resilience?' *Mindmatters Newsletter*, March, p 2.

Canfield, J. and Siccone, F. (1995) *101 Ways to Develop Student Self-esteem and Responsibility*, Allyn and Bacon, Massachusetts.

Cantor, R., Kivel, P. and Creighton, A. (1997) *Days of Respect: Organising a School-wide Violence Prevention Program*, Hunter House, California.

Catalano, R. and Hawkins, J.D. (Ed) (1996) The social development model: a theory of antisocial behaviour. In Hawkins J.D. (Ed) *Delinquency and Crime: Current Theories*, Cambridge Publications, New York.

Centre for Adolescent Health (1998) *The Gatehouse Project: Promoting Emotional Well-being: A Whole-School Approach – Team Guidelines*, Centre for Adolescent Health, Melbourne.

Department of Education, Victoria (1999) *Framework for Student Services in Victorian Schools:* Teacher resource, Department of Education, Victoria.

DfES (2003) *Developing children's social, emotional and behavioural skills: a whole curriculum approach.* Primary National Strategy.

Fuller, A. (1998) *From Surviving to Thriving: Promoting Mental Health in Young People*, ACER Press, Melbourne.

Fuller, A., McGraw, K. and Goodyear, M. (1998) *The Mind of Youth*, Department of Education, Melbourne, Australia.

Fuller, A. (2001) Background Paper on Resilience presented to the Northern Territory Principal's Association (Australia).

Goleman, D. (1995) *Emotional Intelligence – Why it matters more than IQ*, London, Bloomsbury.

Hawkins, J. and Catalano, R. (1993) *Communities that Care: Risk and Protective Focused Prevention Using the Social Development Strategy*, Developmental Research and Programs Incorporated, Seattle, USA.

Lickona, T. (1997) 'Educating for Character: a comprehensive approach' in A. Molnar (ed.), *The Construction of Children's Character*, University of Chicago Press, Chicago.

Olweus, D. (1995) *Bullying or Peer Abuse at School – facts and interventions*, Current Directions in Psychological Science, 4,6, p 196-200.

Resnick, M.D., Harris, L.J. and Blum, R.W. (1993) *The impact of caring and connectedness on adolescent health and wellbeing*, Journal of Paediatrics and Child Health, 29.

Rigby, K. (1996) *Bullying in schools and what we can do about it.* ACER Press, Melbourne, Australia.

Seligman, M. (1995) *The Optimistic Child*, NSW, Random House, Australia.

Smith, C. and McKee, S. (2005) *Becoming an Emotionally Healthy School*, A Lucky Duck Book, Paul Chapman, London.

Taylor, M. (2000) 'Values Education: Issues and challenges in policy and school practice' in M. Leicester, C. Modgil and S. Modgil (ed.), *Education, Culture and Values*, Vol 2. Falmer Press, London.